Pitch and Throw, Grasp and Know

What Is a Synonym?

To my brother Danny—
the wordsmith of the family

—B.P.C.

Synonym:
A word that
has the same or
nearly the same
meaning as
another word

Pitch and Throw, Grasp and Know

What Is a Synonym?

by Brian P. Cleary

illustrated by Brian Gable

M MILLBROOK PRESS / MINNEAPOLIS

Do you feel tired
or **beat**
or **exhausted**

from making the cake
that you've baked
and you've frosted?

from a whole list of possible words you can use.

They're words that are *practically, nearly* the same,

by letting us choose between blue plates or dishes.

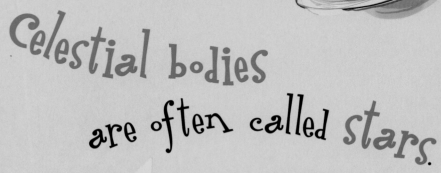

Celestial bodies are often called stars.

Streets can be avenues.
Autos are cars.

Synonyms
help us to be
more exact,

like, nippy
or freezing
or chilly as ice.

comprehend
and grasp
and know.

Yell and holler.

Jump
and
leap.

SYNONYM

Fly and soar,

and doze and sleep.

Richness and depth are what **synonyms** raise

When they're used in a paragraph, sentence, or phrase.

A lovely and pretty and beautiful city.

Cat
Feline
Kitty

A cat
or a feline
could be called a kitty.

They let us pick showering, raining, or pouring.

Without them,
our language would
surely be boring!

for the sneakers
or tennis shoes,

yellow or golden.

ABOUT THE AUTHOR & ILLUSTRATOR

BRIAN P. CLEARY is the author of the Words Are CATegorical©, Math Is CATegorical©, Food Is CATegorical™, Adventures in Memory™, and Sounds Like Reading™ series. He has also written The Laugh Stand: Adventures in Humor; Peanut Butter and Jellyfishes: A Very Silly Alphabet Book; The Punctuation Station; and two poetry books. Mr. Cleary lives in Cleveland, Ohio.

BRIAN GABLE is the illustrator of several Words Are CATegorical© books, as well as the Math Is CATegorical© series. Mr. Gable also works as a political cartoonist for the Globe and Mail newspaper in Toronto, Canada.

Text copyright © 2005 by Brian P. Cleary
Illustrations copyright © 2005 by Lerner Publishing Group, Inc.

Millbrook Press
A division of Lerner Publishing Group, Inc.
241 First Avenue North
Minneapolis, MN 55401 U.S.A.

Website address: www.lernerbooks.com

Library of Congress Cataloging-in-Publication Data

Cleary, Brian P., 1959-
  Pitch and throw, grasp and know : what is a synonym? / by Brian P. Cleary; illustrated by Brian Gable.
    p.   cm. — (Words are categorical)
   ISBN 978-1-57505-796-5 (lib. bdg. : alk. paper)
   ISBN 978-1-57505-907-5 (eBook)
   1. English language—Synonyms and antonyms—Juvenile literature. I. Gable, Brian, 1949- II. Title. III. Series.
PE1591.C56 2005
   428.1—dc22   2004011975

Manufactured in the United States of America
9 — CG — 4/1/13